Name   : ....

Address :...

Email   :...
.

Phone Number :.................................

Gift Certificate Log

No.	Issue Date	Recipient	Amount	Expire Date	Date Redeemed

Gift Certificate Log

No.	Issue Date	Recipient	Amount	Expire Date	Date Redeemed

Gift Certificate Log

No.	Issue Date	Recipient	Amount	Expire Date	Date Redeemed

Gift Certificate Log

No.	Issue Date	Recipient	Amount	Expire Date	Date Redeemed

Gift Certificate Log

No.	Issue Date	Recipient	Amount	Expire Date	Date Redeemed

Gift Certificate Log

No.	Issue Date	Recipient	Amount	Expire Date	Date Redeemed

Gift Certificate Log

No.	Issue Date	Recipient	Amount	Expire Date	Date Redeemed

Gift Certificate Log

No.	Issue Date	Recipient	Amount	Expire Date	Date Redeemed

Gift Certificate Log

No.	Issue Date	Recipient	Amount	Expire Date	Date Redeemed

Gift Certificate Log

No.	Issue Date	Recipient	Amount	Expire Date	Date Redeemed

Gift Certificate Log

No.	Issue Date	Recipient	Amount	Expire Date	Date Redeemed

Gift Certificate Log

No.	Issue Date	Recipient	Amount	Expire Date	Date Redeemed

Gift Certificate Log

No.	Issue Date	Recipient	Amount	Expire Date	Date Redeemed

Gift Certificate Log

No.	Issue Date	Recipient	Amount	Expire Date	Date Redeemed

Gift Certificate Log

No.	Issue Date	Recipient	Amount	Expire Date	Date Redeemed

Gift Certificate Log

No.	Issue Date	Recipient	Amount	Expire Date	Date Redeemed

Gift Certificate Log

No.	Issue Date	Recipient	Amount	Expire Date	Date Redeemed

Gift Certificate Log

No.	Issue Date	Recipient	Amount	Expire Date	Date Redeemed

Gift Certificate Log

No.	Issue Date	Recipient	Amount	Expire Date	Date Redeemed

Gift Certificate Log

No.	Issue Date	Recipient	Amount	Expire Date	Date Redeemed

Gift Certificate Log

No.	Issue Date	Recipient	Amount	Expire Date	Date Redeemed

Gift Certificate Log

No.	Issue Date	Recipient	Amount	Expire Date	Date Redeemed

Gift Certificate Log

No.	Issue Date	Recipient	Amount	Expire Date	Date Redeemed

Gift Certificate Log

No.	Issue Date	Recipient	Amount	Expire Date	Date Redeemed

Gift Certificate Log

No.	Issue Date	Recipient	Amount	Expire Date	Date Redeemed

Gift Certificate Log

No.	Issue Date	Recipient	Amount	Expire Date	Date Redeemed

Gift Certificate Log

No.	Issue Date	Recipient	Amount	Expire Date	Date Redeemed

Gift Certificate Log

No.	Issue Date	Recipient	Amount	Expire Date	Date Redeemed

Gift Certificate Log

No.	Issue Date	Recipient	Amount	Expire Date	Date Redeemed

Gift Certificate Log

No.	Issue Date	Recipient	Amount	Expire Date	Date Redeemed

Gift Certificate Log

No.	Issue Date	Recipient	Amount	Expire Date	Date Redeemed

Gift Certificate Log

No.	Issue Date	Recipient	Amount	Expire Date	Date Redeemed

Gift Certificate Log

No.	Issue Date	Recipient	Amount	Expire Date	Date Redeemed

Gift Certificate Log

No.	Issue Date	Recipient	Amount	Expire Date	Date Redeemed

Gift Certificate Log

No.	Issue Date	Recipient	Amount	Expire Date	Date Redeemed

Gift Certificate Log

No.	Issue Date	Recipient	Amount	Expire Date	Date Redeemed

Gift Certificate Log

No.	Issue Date	Recipient	Amount	Expire Date	Date Redeemed

Gift Certificate Log

No.	Issue Date	Recipient	Amount	Expire Date	Date Redeemed

Gift Certificate Log

No.	Issue Date	Recipient	Amount	Expire Date	Date Redeemed

Gift Certificate Log

No.	Issue Date	Recipient	Amount	Expire Date	Date Redeemed

Gift Certificate Log

No.	Issue Date	Recipient	Amount	Expire Date	Date Redeemed

Gift Certificate Log

No.	Issue Date	Recipient	Amount	Expire Date	Date Redeemed

Gift Certificate Log

No.	Issue Date	Recipient	Amount	Expire Date	Date Redeemed

Gift Certificate Log

No.	Issue Date	Recipient	Amount	Expire Date	Date Redeemed

Gift Certificate Log

No.	Issue Date	Recipient	Amount	Expire Date	Date Redeemed

Gift Certificate Log

No.	Issue Date	Recipient	Amount	Expire Date	Date Redeemed

Gift Certificate Log

No.	Issue Date	Recipient	Amount	Expire Date	Date Redeemed

Gift Certificate Log

No.	Issue Date	Recipient	Amount	Expire Date	Date Redeemed

Gift Certificate Log

No.	Issue Date	Recipient	Amount	Expire Date	Date Redeemed

Gift Certificate Log

No.	Issue Date	Recipient	Amount	Expire Date	Date Redeemed

Gift Certificate Log

No.	Issue Date	Recipient	Amount	Expire Date	Date Redeemed

Gift Certificate Log

No.	Issue Date	Recipient	Amount	Expire Date	Date Redeemed

Gift Certificate Log

No.	Issue Date	Recipient	Amount	Expire Date	Date Redeemed

Gift Certificate Log

No.	Issue Date	Recipient	Amount	Expire Date	Date Redeemed

Gift Certificate Log

No.	Issue Date	Recipient	Amount	Expire Date	Date Redeemed

Gift Certificate Log

No.	Issue Date	Recipient	Amount	Expire Date	Date Redeemed

Gift Certificate Log

No.	Issue Date	Recipient	Amount	Expire Date	Date Redeemed

Gift Certificate Log

No.	Issue Date	Recipient	Amount	Expire Date	Date Redeemed

Gift Certificate Log

No.	Issue Date	Recipient	Amount	Expire Date	Date Redeemed

Gift Certificate Log

No.	Issue Date	Recipient	Amount	Expire Date	Date Redeemed

Gift Certificate Log

No.	Issue Date	Recipient	Amount	Expire Date	Date Redeemed

Gift Certificate Log

No.	Issue Date	Recipient	Amount	Expire Date	Date Redeemed

Gift Certificate Log

No.	Issue Date	Recipient	Amount	Expire Date	Date Redeemed

Gift Certificate Log

No.	Issue Date	Recipient	Amount	Expire Date	Date Redeemed

Gift Certificate Log

No.	Issue Date	Recipient	Amount	Expire Date	Date Redeemed

Gift Certificate Log

No.	Issue Date	Recipient	Amount	Expire Date	Date Redeemed

Gift Certificate Log

No.	Issue Date	Recipient	Amount	Expire Date	Date Redeemed

Gift Certificate Log

No.	Issue Date	Recipient	Amount	Expire Date	Date Redeemed

Gift Certificate Log

No.	Issue Date	Recipient	Amount	Expire Date	Date Redeemed

Gift Certificate Log

No.	Issue Date	Recipient	Amount	Expire Date	Date Redeemed

Gift Certificate Log

No.	Issue Date	Recipient	Amount	Expire Date	Date Redeemed

Gift Certificate Log

No.	Issue Date	Recipient	Amount	Expire Date	Date Redeemed

Gift Certificate Log

No.	Issue Date	Recipient	Amount	Expire Date	Date Redeemed

Gift Certificate Log

No.	Issue Date	Recipient	Amount	Expire Date	Date Redeemed

Gift Certificate Log

No.	Issue Date	Recipient	Amount	Expire Date	Date Redeemed

Gift Certificate Log

No.	Issue Date	Recipient	Amount	Expire Date	Date Redeemed

Gift Certificate Log

No.	Issue Date	Recipient	Amount	Expire Date	Date Redeemed

Gift Certificate Log

No.	Issue Date	Recipient	Amount	Expire Date	Date Redeemed

Gift Certificate Log

No.	Issue Date	Recipient	Amount	Expire Date	Date Redeemed

Gift Certificate Log

No.	Issue Date	Recipient	Amount	Expire Date	Date Redeemed

Gift Certificate Log

No.	Issue Date	Recipient	Amount	Expire Date	Date Redeemed

Gift Certificate Log

No.	Issue Date	Recipient	Amount	Expire Date	Date Redeemed

Gift Certificate Log

No.	Issue Date	Recipient	Amount	Expire Date	Date Redeemed

Gift Certificate Log

No.	Issue Date	Recipient	Amount	Expire Date	Date Redeemed

Gift Certificate Log

No.	Issue Date	Recipient	Amount	Expire Date	Date Redeemed

Gift Certificate Log

No.	Issue Date	Recipient	Amount	Expire Date	Date Redeemed

Gift Certificate Log

No.	Issue Date	Recipient	Amount	Expire Date	Date Redeemed

Gift Certificate Log

No.	Issue Date	Recipient	Amount	Expire Date	Date Redeemed

Gift Certificate Log

No.	Issue Date	Recipient	Amount	Expire Date	Date Redeemed

Gift Certificate Log

No.	Issue Date	Recipient	Amount	Expire Date	Date Redeemed

Gift Certificate Log

No.	Issue Date	Recipient	Amount	Expire Date	Date Redeemed

Gift Certificate Log

No.	Issue Date	Recipient	Amount	Expire Date	Date Redeemed

Gift Certificate Log

No.	Issue Date	Recipient	Amount	Expire Date	Date Redeemed

Gift Certificate Log

No.	Issue Date	Recipient	Amount	Expire Date	Date Redeemed

Gift Certificate Log

No.	Issue Date	Recipient	Amount	Expire Date	Date Redeemed

Gift Certificate Log

No.	Issue Date	Recipient	Amount	Expire Date	Date Redeemed

Gift Certificate Log

No.	Issue Date	Recipient	Amount	Expire Date	Date Redeemed

Gift Certificate Log

No.	Issue Date	Recipient	Amount	Expire Date	Date Redeemed

Gift Certificate Log

No.	Issue Date	Recipient	Amount	Expire Date	Date Redeemed

Made in the USA
Coppell, TX
17 December 2024

42595381R00057